Zoom™ In on
Ocean Animals

Dolphins

Leo Statts

abdopublishing.com

Published by Abdo Zoom™, PO Box 398166, Minneapolis, Minnesota 55439. Copyright © 2017 by Abdo Consulting Group, Inc. International copyrights reserved in all countries. No part of this book may be reproduced in any form without written permission from the publisher. Abdo Zoom™ is a trademark and logo of Abdo Consulting Group, Inc.

Printed in the United States of America, North Mankato, Minnesota
092016
012017

Cover Photo: Paulphin Photography/Shutterstock Images
Interior Photos: iStockphoto, 1, 7, 10–11, 16; Andrea Izzotti/iStockphoto, 4; Shin Okamoto/iStockphoto, 6–7; Krzysztof Odziomek/iStockphoto, 8; Amit Erez/iStockphoto, 9; Red Line Editorial, 11, 20 (left), 20 (right), 21 (left), 21 (right); David Schrader/iStockphoto, 12–13; Targn Pleiades/Shutterstock Images, 15; Matt Jeacock/iStockphoto, 17; Thurston Photo/iStockphoto, 19

Editor: Brienna Rossiter
Series Designer: Madeline Berger
Art Direction: Dorothy Toth

Publisher's Cataloging-in-Publication Data
Names: Statts, Leo, author.
Title: Dolphins / by Leo Statts.
Description: Minneapolis, MN : Abdo Zoom, 2017. | Series: Ocean animals |
      Includes bibliographical references and index.
Identifiers: LCCN 2016948671 | ISBN 9781680799118 (lib. bdg.) |
      ISBN 9781624024979 (ebook) | ISBN 9781624025532 (Read-to-me ebook)
Subjects: LCSH: Dolphins--Juvenile literature.
Classification: DDC 599.53--dc23
LC record available at http://lccn.loc.gov/2016948671

Table of Contents

Dolphins

Dolphins are **mammals**.
They are a kind of whale.

There are more than 30 kinds of dolphins. Bottlenose dolphins are the most common.

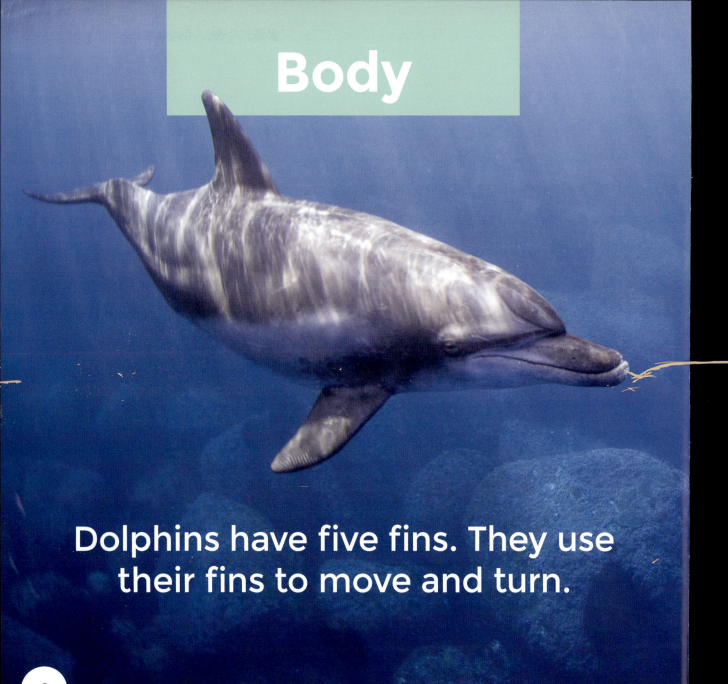

Body

Dolphins have five fins. They use their fins to move and turn.

They use their fins to jump
out of the water, too.

A dolphin has a long snout.

A blowhole is on top of
the dolphin's head.
The dolphin uses it to breathe.

Habitat

Dolphins live in oceans around the world. Some live in rivers, too. You can often find them in **shallow** water.

■ Where dolphins live

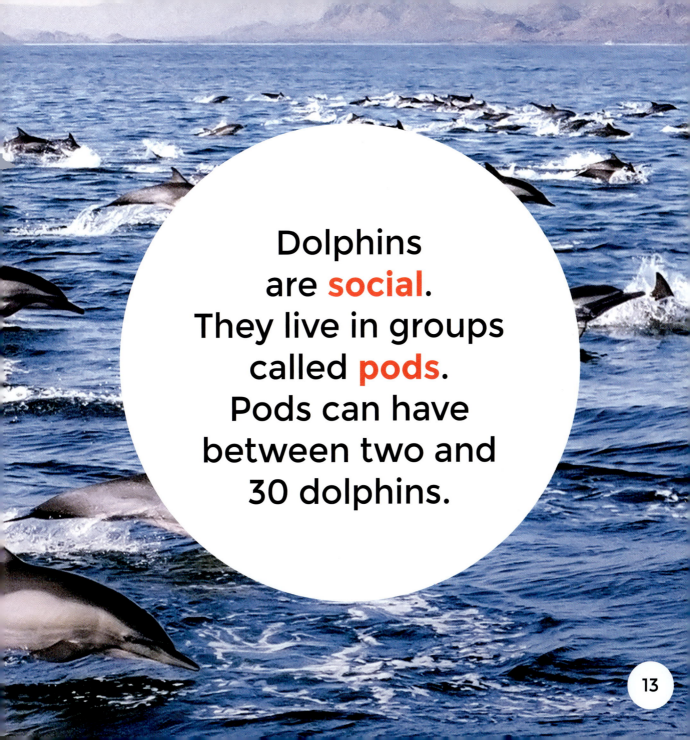

Dolphins are **social**. They live in groups called **pods**. Pods can have between two and 30 dolphins.

Food

Dolphins eat fish, squid, and crabs. The dolphins in a pod hunt together. They take turns catching fish.

Life Cycle

Dolphins have live babies.
They have one baby at a time.

Calves stay with their mothers for up to eight years.

Some dolphins live around 20 years. Others can live to be 70 years old.

Most Common Length

A bottlenose dolphin
is longer than a sofa.

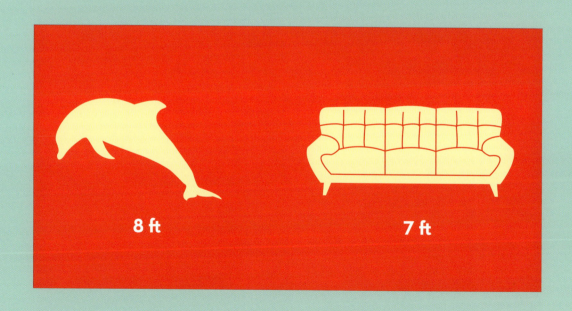

8 ft

7 ft

Smallest Length

A Maui's dolphin is longer than an acoustic guitar.

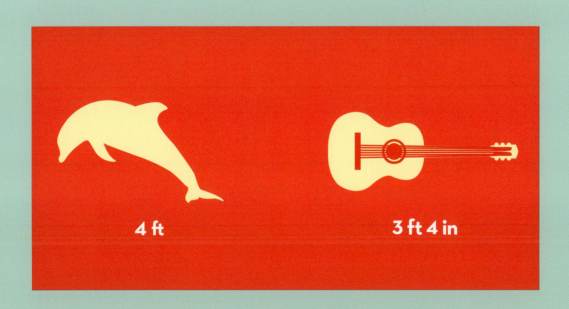

4 ft

3 ft 4 in

Glossary

calves - baby animals.

mammal - an animal that makes milk to feed its young and usually has hair or fur.

pod - a group of dolphins or whales.

shallow - not deep.

snout - a part of the face that sticks out. It has the nose and mouth.

social - friendly; enjoys being around others.

Booklinks

For more information
on **dolphins**, please visit
booklinks.abdopublishing.com

Z⊙⊙m **In on Animals!**

Learn even more with the Abdo Zoom
Animals database. Check out
abdozoom.com for more information.

Index